Contents

Acknowledgments

First and foremost, I want to thank my wife Linda who has been there for me the whole way though this journey. Linda, you have always believed in me and strengthened me when I doubted the value of what God has given me. You are my number one fan, and I owe everything to you.

I also want to share my gratitude for my brother and sister, Joey and Learsi. You two never let this dream die in me. Many times, you have heard me teaching in your kitchen, your car, and the many places we have been together. It may not have seemed so then, but I have heard you every time you said, "You need to write that down."

To my supporting family of Una Iglesia, who have tirelessly prayed for me and this work. Thank you for bugging me and challenging me to the point where it was impossible for me to give up. Thank you all so much for your prayers and support.

I must mention the origin of my encouragement to write. To the one who took me to all of the doctors' appointments, tutors, and special help classes—the one who would not take no for an answer—who said, "There must be a solution to his struggles with learning." From learning disabilities to autism to dyslexia, you covered it all. Whatever it took, you did it for me because you believed that I had great things in me. I have never, nor will I ever forget all the things you did for me. You promoted me, defended me, and most of all, you loved me. e When I graduated from high school, and I tested for college reading and writing at a second-grade level; when my counselors and coaches told me that I was not college material; when I was not accepted to any university because of my low test scores; and when I was required to pass several remedial courses without college credit just to be able to take the courses that were for credit. Even with all of this and much more, you never wavered in your convictions about me. You never gave up.

I know you are in heaven looking down on me even now. I know that God allowed you to see your dreams come true. I know He is kind and has let you see. He is so good that He allowed me to honor you and without even knowing it. For the benefit of the reader, I will share the story that you already know. I finished writing the manuscript of this book on January 7th. I came out of my office looking for my wife, Linda. "Babe!" I called out. Linda approached me from our kitchen, and with a grand smile and open arms, I said, "I am finished. I am done with the book." Linda, smiling from ear to ear, said, "Do you know what today is?" I thought to myself, *What an odd question?* Sarcastically I said, "It's Thursday." Linda said, "Yes, and today is your mom's anniversary." Linda was speaking of my mom's death as she had died on January 7th. I paused and said, "No, Mom was born on this day, and she is celebrating with us." Her dream has finally come true. Thank you, Mom.

Introduction

The world can be a tough place to live. At one time or another, we are all faced with difficult challenges in our lives. Life begins with crying. The first achievement from the womb is to cry. As a newborn, this first life experience is terribly traumatic, but to its parents, it is like beautiful music. In our beginning, the simple act of breathing must be attained so that we can continue with life. Our screaming is the way of passage. The second achievement in life is to express displeasure with being hungry. The satisfaction of a full belly is quickly followed by giving back waste materials without shame and a nice nap. The level of life's troubles are relative to where we are on our journey through it. As we mature, our troubles only shift to other things.

No matter what the dilemma, it is always comforting to hear of someone who can relate to the situations that we face. Take, for example, someone who is preparing to attend college. This can be frightening, but an inspiring story, of those who have overcome personal challenges to achieve an education, provides encouragement. On the other hand, it is disheartening to speak with someone who cannot relate. A typical reply is, "You don't understand..." No one should be faulted because they have not had the same experiences that you have had. Is it possible for anyone who has never lost a loved one or faced death to understand what these trials are like? We have all experienced those who are well intended, but they cannot possibly understand.

Troubles are a part of life. Isn't it interesting that when we are in the midst of trouble, we feel that it is the most difficult situation anyone has ever faced? Many times, we think we are the only ones who have gone through the difficulty. After the troubled time passes, we can't remember having gone through the problem in the first place.

A difficult situation is exactly what brought me to write this work. Several years ago, even though I cannot tell you what it was about, I was going through a trying time. I felt like the whole world was coming down on me, and no one could possibly understand what I was going through. I thought, "These things only happen to me," even though I knew this was not the case. There I was, deep into the middle of my tragedy, that now, I can't even remember.

I had come in from school, and I was lying in my bed. It felt like forever that I laid there, staring at the ceiling. I probably set some kind of record for the longest time without blinking. It was me and my thoughts; over and over. I don't remember why I was there, but I vividly remember this part: with my eyebrows together and my lips pouting, I exclaimed to God, "You don't know what this is like! You are up there, and I am down here. Where You are is perfect, but it is not perfect down here." What was I saying to Him? I was saying that He does not know what it is like to have to endure the things that I endure. This rant of mine was short-lived. I became silent as I heard the Lord say to me in my heart, "I do know, and I am mindful because I know." "How do You know, Lord?" I questioned. How can He be up there and know what it is like to be me down here?

This writing was born out of this experience. Up until this point, I had only seen God as Almighty God. This is what I had been taught. However, in this moment, I realized, that Jesus had come to earth as a man. He was born, lived, and died. I knew these facts, but I had completely missed that Jesus was a man (human) like me. Maybe His path was not exactly like ours, but He lived here just like you and I do. Just like us, Jesus faced troubles in life. Jesus was fully God, but He was also fully man. He understands what this life is because He lived it.

Seeing Jesus as human helped me to connect with Him in a whole new way. Jesus became personal to me, and I came to appreciate that Jesus does relate to me on a personal level. Before He was sent to earth, Jesus was already perfect in every way. Jesus, as a human, came in the likeness of you and I. Jesus' empathy for you in your humanity is genuine. On your behalf, Jesus endured this world, and He triumphed over it. Take comfort that you have a Savior who understands. He understands because He has faced the same things you do, and He has overcome them all.

Study Help

Whether you read this book weekly, for a year, or randomly as the need arises, the approach is the same. Each reflection begins with a simple question, and each question has a Yes or No answer. Begin by reading the question and then stop. Ponder the question that you have just been asked. Before you continue reading, try to think of one or more experiences in your own life. For example, the question may be, "Have you ever had to take a test?" If you answer Yes, then take some time to remember these experiences before you continue reading. If you struggle to come up with an example, don't worry about it. Continue reading to see if the next segment will help you.

After each question, you will find a series of examples that have occurred for others. Use these examples to think further about your own life. It may be a situation that is current or from your past. It is not important when the experiences happened, but it is key that the experiences are yours. Relating to experiences of others for inspiration is a good start, but this is about you.

Next, you will find a Bible verse. When you read the verse, think human. Think of the person, the human, who is experiencing the situation presented in the verse. Even if you have not had an exact experience of the one presented in the verse, think about how you would react if you were the person going through it. How would you feel? What would you do in this situation? It is important to connect your life experiences with the person being described in the verse. After the verse, there are further insights on the verse to give it context.

The person in the Bible verse is always Jesus. It is a beautiful thing to realize that you and the Savior of the world have had similar experiences. Jesus can look you in the eye and say, "I know how you feel." When He says, "Come, let me help you." You will know that He empathizes with you, and His help is true.

Now that we have reflected on our lives, let's pray. Pray the prayer with me, and I encourage you to continue praying on your own. Talk to Jesus like you would a best friend. Jesus is God, but He is also one who understands.

The next section of the reflection is a personal journal. It is for you to write whatever you want. There is no right or wrong answers. Personal journaling can be intimidating as digging into the dark places of our lives can be tough, especially when it hurts. Remember, the Holy Spirit will go with you. Jesus sent the Holy Spirit to teach and strengthen you.

Each journal has a similar starting point. The goal is to help you: 1) remember, 2) face how you felt, 3) be honest how you react, and 4) what can be different. The journal is yours, and it will be as much or as little as you make it. Give it a try for a week, and ask the Holy Spirit to help you. You'll be amazed at what you may find. Here, I will help you. Prayer: "Holy Spirit, please help me. Go with me on this journey, and teach me along the way. I want to learn, and I want to have the better life that Jesus talked about. Amen." See how easy that was? Life is different when the Holy Spirit is active in your life.

Each reflection ends with a verse of encouragement. The verse given is not intended to answer everything, but is rather a seed for hope for a fresh start. Jesus and His Holy Spirit are required for daily life. As you begin to believe differently, you will begin to think differently. As you think differently, you will act differently, and your life will begin to take on a whole new meaning.

Reflections

The term *reflection* is defined by Oxford Dictionaries as "serious thought or consideration." As you read each reflection, take the time to think about yourself, Jesus, and how similar the two of you really are. As you come to connect Jesus' daily battles with your own, you will see why He understands You. Jesus won over all of life's trials, and He has provided you with His Holy Spirit to lead you to the same victory.

Time for Yourself | 1

Have you ever wanted some time for yourself? A few minutes would be nice. Maybe you want to take a warm bath or go out for a short walk, but you could not because your kids, work, bills, or something unexpected demanded your time. Life has obligations. Many of them are required, but most of them are not. We often commit ourselves to things that would be better left alone. From time to time, it is good to take a few minutes for yourself, but often life's demands prevent you. Whatever the reason, being absorbed by life can leave you out of gas. Mark 7:24: "Jesus got up and went away from there to the region of Tyre. And when He had entered a house, He wanted no one to know of it; yet He could not escape notice." What this means is that Jesus understands what it is like to work long hours, and He wanted some time alone. Yes, Jesus wanted some quiet time, but some days, even He could not find a place to relax . He intended to go into the house in hopes that no one would know He was there, but they found Him anyway. You guessed it, He was found, and they began to demand more of His time. Take comfort that you have a Savior who understands. He understands because He has faced the same things you do, and He has overcome them all.

He could not find a place to relax

Prayer: Lord, I know that taking some time for myself helps me. Please help me to better manage my time, so I can rest and refuel. Amen.

Journal: Time or No Time

When I think about taking some time for myself, I feel

_____

_____

_____

_____

_____

_____

When I am unable to take time for myself, I react by

_____

_____

_____

_____

_____

_____

_____

_____

When I need time for myself, I will

_____

_____

_____

_____

_____

_____

Encouragement: When you are done working, rest (Genesis 2:2).

Unbelievable | 2

Have you ever had someone refuse to believe you? You did everything you could to convince them that you are telling them the truth, but no matter what, they will not believe you. Maybe your spouse, boss, friend, or family member believed you did something that you did not do. Maybe you have tried to encourage a fearful child to jump into a swimming pool, but nothing you did persuaded the child to jump in. Maybe, drawing from your experience in a matter, you gave someone solid advice, but they did not listen. Because they did not believe you, they suffered the heartache you warned them about. Whatever the reason, not being believed can be frustrating. John 12:37: "But though He had performed so many signs before them, yet they were not believing in Him." What this means is that Jesus understands what it is like to not be believed. Even with all the spectacular works that Jesus performed, some people just would not believe in Him. Imagine that it was you who had performed the miracles Jesus did, and they still would not believe in you. These people had determined in their hearts to reject Jesus, so they were unable to receive from Him. Because they refused Him, Jesus could not help them. Take comfort that you have a Savior who understands. He understands because He has faced the same things you do, and He has overcome them all.

people just would not believe in Him

Prayer: Lord, I don't know why sometimes people don't believe what I say. Please help me to stay true to myself and remember that You believe me. Let this be enough. Amen.

Journal: Believe or Not

When someone does not believe me, I feel _____

_____

_____

_____

_____

_____

_____

_____

_____

When I am doubted, I react by _____

_____

_____

_____

_____

_____

_____

_____

When I am not believed, I will _____

_____

_____

_____

_____

_____

_____

_____

Encouragement: Say your "Yes" or "No," and say no more (James 5:12).

Hungry | 3

Have you ever been crazy hungry? You were starving, but you could not find anything to eat. Maybe you were on a long trip, and all of the eating establishments were closed. Maybe you wanted a snack from the snack machine, but it was broken. This can sound insignificant, but hunger can drive you to do some pretty abnormal things. Whatever the reason, hunger can make you a little cranky and cause you to do or say things you later regret.

the snack machine Matthew 21:18: "Now in the morning, when He was returning to the city, He became hungry." What this means is that Jesus understands what it is like to feel hunger just like you do. Continuing to read this Scripture, you will see that Jesus walked over to a fig tree, which was the snack machine of His time. The tree looked like it should have figs, but there were none. Even with this, Jesus took this opportunity to teach His disciples. Take comfort that you have a Savior who understands. He understands because He has faced the same things you do, and He has overcome them all.

Prayer: : Lord, sometimes when I get hungry, I say and do things that I don't mean. Please help me to be kind even when I struggle. Amen.

Journal: Hungry or Full

When I am hungry, I feel
_____
_____
_____
_____
_____
_____
_____

When I am hungry, I react by
_____
_____
_____
_____
_____
_____
_____

When I become hungry, I will
_____
_____
_____
_____
_____
_____
_____
_____

Encouragement: God satisfies (Proverbs 10:3).

Sleep | 4

Have you ever been without a place to sleep? Maybe you have lost your home, or your car broke down in a strange place. Maybe you were stuck in a town with no hotel vacancies. It is disheartening to be faced with sleeping without the protection of a home or a family. Where will you go? How can you stay safe? Maybe you have always had a place to sleep, but you do not sleep peacefully. Your mind runs wild as you try to rest. Whatever the reason, not being able to rest well can be physically and

all alone, mentally draining. Matthew 8:20: "Jesus said
with no place to him, 'The foxes have holes and the birds
to sleep of the air have nests, but the Son of Man has nowhere to lay His head.'" What this means understands what a it is like to have nowhere to sleep. Jesus' path forward was a hard one. He had traveled this same way many times before, and He was invited to stay with the people. This time, Jesus was no longer welcome. He saw the houses that welcomed Him in the past, yet He was all alone, with no place to sleep. Take comfort that you have a Savior who understands. He understands because He has faced the same things you do, and He has overcome them all.

Prayer: Lord, whatever the reason, I am unable to rest, I give my unrest to You. I pray that You will be my peace and my shelter. Amen.

Journal: Unrest or Peaceful

When I am unable to sleep, I feel

_____

_____

_____

_____

_____

_____

_____

When I lose too much sleep, I react by

_____

_____

_____

_____

_____

_____

_____

When I become restless, I will

_____

_____

_____

_____

_____

_____

_____

Encouragement: Go to sleep. You are safe (Psalm 4:8).

Standing Alone | 5

Have you ever been left standing alone? Maybe you were facing a breakup or lost your job. Exactly when you needed a friend the most, no one was to be found. You expect that the people closest to you will stand by your side when times get tough, but sometimes no one is there for you. When you find yourself all alone your only remaining choice for a friend is God, if you choose to receive Him. Whatever the reason, being left alone can leave you feeling abandoned and empty.

they all left Him

John 16:32: "Behold, an hour is coming, and has already come, for you to be scattered, each to his own home, and to leave Me alone; and yet I am not alone, because the Father is with Me."

What this means is that Jesus understands what it is like to have those who were closest to Him leave Him all by Himself, the very people that Jesus poured Himself into. The ones who said that they would be with Him to the end; they all left Him. Jesus faced His most difficult circumstances of His life alone. Take comfort that you have a Savior who understands. He understands because He has faced the same things you do, and He has overcome them all.

Prayer: Lord, I don't like it when those I thought I could trust leave me standing alone. Please help me to forgive those who have left me, and help me to remember that You will never leave me alone. Amen.

Journal: Alone or Together

When I am left standing alone, I feel
_____
_____
_____
_____
_____
_____

When I am left standing alone, I react by
_____
_____
_____
_____
_____
_____

When I find myself left alone, I will
_____
_____
_____
_____
_____
_____
_____

Encouragement: You are stuck with Him (Deuteronomy 31:6).

The Agony | 6

Have you ever been deeply sad? You were so distressed that you just wanted to curl up and die. Maybe you lost a loved one, a child or a great friend. Maybe you lost everything you owned. Maybe you lost your job or even faced losing your life. At some point in life, you will most likely encounter conditions that make you feel that there is no hope. All you want is for the trouble you are facing to be over with. Sometimes, things cause so much misery that they can make you want to take your own life. You just want the trouble ended so you can find peace again. Whatever the reason, being deeply saddened can be devastating. Matthew 26:38: "Then He said to them, 'My soul is deeply grieved, to the point of death; remain here and keep watch with Me.'" What this means is that Jesus understands what it is like to suffer. It was such a trying time in His life that it felt like it was going to kill Him. His heart was breaking as He faced punishment, death, and the abandonment of His Father. Yes, even His Dad left Him. Through prayer, Jesus found the strength to persevere. Take comfort that you have a Savior who understands. He understands because He has faced the same things you do, and He has overcome them all.

even His Dad left Him

Prayer: Lord, my grief has overcome me. Please help me find joy again. Amen.

Journal: Grief or Joy

I feel sad when

_____

_____

_____

_____

_____

_____

_____

When I am sad, I react by

_____

_____

_____

_____

_____

_____

_____

When I am becoming sad, I will

_____

_____

_____

_____

_____

_____

_____

Encouragement: He fixes broken hearts (Psalm 34:18).

Don't Want To | 7

Have you ever had to do something that you did not want to do? Maybe you have been faced with an extremely difficult challenge, like going to court. Maybe you had to take a test that would determine if you would pass or fail. Maybe you have faced a life-threatening treatment for an illness. It is natural to search for a better way, but many times, no alternative can be found. Whatever the reason, being faced with challenges we do not want to do can be truly stressful. Matthew 26:39: "And He went a little beyond them, and fell on His face and prayed, saying, 'My Father, if it is possible, let this cup pass from Me; yet not as I will, but as You will.'" What this means is that Jesus understands what it is like to surrender His will to the plan of Father God. He had to put his desires aside because it was not possible for the Father to provide another way for Jesus to complete His will. Jesus knew that He was destined to die while carrying our sin. Even His Father would have to turn away from Him. Take comfort that you have a Savior who understands. He understands because He has faced the same things you do, and He has overcome them all.

He had to put his desires aside

Prayer: Lord, some things that I am required to do I simply do not want to do. Please help me to receive Your strength and peace. Amen.

Journal: Do or Don't

When I am required to do or say something that I do not
want to, I feel

_____

_____

_____

_____

_____

_____

When I am not in control, I react by

_____

_____

_____

_____

_____

_____

When I must do something I do not prefer, I will

_____

_____

_____

_____

_____

_____

Encouragement: It's already done; just go (Isaiah 45:2).

Tempted | 8

Have you ever been enticed into doing something you knew was not right? Maybe you have started a diet, and late at night, that slice of cake in your refrigerator calls out to you. Maybe you have been short of money, and after you finished shopping, you discovered the cashier did not charge you for some of the items you had. No one will notice them missing. It appears impossible to resist the temptation when it comes, and this is especially true

At His lowest point when you are in times of weakness. Whatever the reason, being tempted takes character to overcome. John 4:1: "Then Jesus was led up by the Spirit into the wilderness to be tempted by the devil." What this means is that Jesus understands what it is like to be tempted. Jesus became weak because He had gone without eating for some forty days. At His lowest point, the tempter offered Jesus suggestions for relief. With Jesus, the tempter's plot was unsuccessful because Jesus remembered the truth spoken by His Father (God). Take comfort that you have a Savior who understands. He understands because He has faced the same things you do, and He has overcome them all.

Prayer: Lord, sometimes I don't have the strength to win over temptation. Please help me to know the truth about the results of my choices; help me to receive the power to do what is good. Amen.

Journal: Decline or Accept

When I am tempted with _____, I feel _____
                          (temptation)

_____

_____

_____

_____

_____

_____

When the temptation comes, I react by _____

_____

_____

_____

_____

_____

When I am tempted, I will _____

_____

_____

_____

_____

_____

_____

_____

Encouragement: Take the emergency exit (1 Corinthians 10:13).

My Friend | 9

Have you lost someone? Maybe you had a friend or loved one die. Enduring the death of a family member or friend is an excruciatingly difficult thing to face. The more significant a person is, the more difficult it is for you to let go. If you feel that their death is the end, then the loss can be too much to bear. Whatever the reason, it is not easy to let go of the ones we love. John 11:14: "So Jesus then said to them plainly, 'Lazarus is dead.'"

Lazarus, died

What this means is that Jesus understands what is like to have a good friend die. Lazarus, died. If you read on, you will see that Jesus cried. The Scripture shares that Jesus was moved by the sadness of Lazarus's loved ones. The crowd expressed in John 11:36, "See how He (Jesus) loved him (Lazarus)!" Take comfort that you have a Savior who understands. He understands because He has faced the same things you do, and He has overcome them all.

Prayer: Lord, my heart is broken. I don't have _____ with
(name)
me anymore. Please hug me, and let me know You are with me. Amen.

Journal: Lost Forever or Moved On

When I think about _____, I feel _____

_____(name)_____

_____

_____

_____

_____

_____

_____

_____

When I think about their passing, I react by _____

_____

_____

_____

_____

_____

_____

_____

When I think of them, I will _____

_____

_____

_____

_____

_____

_____

_____

_____

Encouragement: Never die (John 11:25-26).

Exhausted | 10

Have you ever been worn out? You were so exhausted that you felt like you were going to pass out. Maybe you worked several shifts in a row, or maybe you were tirelessly caring for someone who was ill. Maybe you were caring for a newborn. Life's demands can force you into fatigue. You feel like you can't go another step or you will simply fall over. Whatever the reason, being exhausted can leave you feeling helpless. John 4:6: "And Jacob's well was there. So Jesus, being wearied from His journey, was sitting thus by the well. It was about the sixth hour." What this means is that Jesus understands what is it like to be worn out. Jesus was tired from His travels. It was hot, and He needed a place to sit in the shade. Perhaps He could quench His thirst and take a nap. Jesus was sitting by a well that was full of water, but He didn't have a way to draw water for Himself to drink. That must have been tough. Take comfort that you have a Savior who understands. He understands because He has faced the same things you do, and He has overcome them all.

Prayer: Lord, sometimes I go so hard that I wear myself out. Please help me to better manage my time to find rest. Amen.

Journal: Rest or Keep Going

When I become exhausted, I feel

_____

_____

_____

_____

_____

_____

_____

When I am really tired, I react by

_____

_____

_____

_____

_____

_____

_____

When I am headed for exhaustion, I will

_____

_____

_____

_____

_____

_____

_____

_____

Encouragement: Rest stop (Matthew 11:28).

Racism | 11

Have you ever been discarded because of your race, nationality, or social group? Maybe you come from the farm, and you are expected to be simple-minded. Maybe your social group is not particularly nice, and you are labeled as a criminal too. This seems to be more prevalent today than it ever has been, but prejudice has been around since the beginning of time. People can quickly find a reason to disassociate with you. Whatever the reason, being negatively viewed because of your race is unjust. John 1:46: "Nathanael said to him, 'Can any good thing (referring to Jesus) come out of Nazareth?'" What this means is that Jesus understands what it is like to be looked down on. Jesus was wrongly judged just because He was born a Nazarene. Because Jesus came from Nazareth, He could not possibly be of excellence or of good nature. Take comfort that you have a Savior who understands. He understands because He has faced the same things you do, and He has overcome them all.

not possibly be of excellence

Prayer: Lord, You made me who I am. Please help me to be proud and stand on who You made me. Give me the wisdom to deal with those who are against what You have made. Amen.

Journal: It's My Race to Win

When someone is negative toward me because of my race,
I feel
_____
_____
_____
_____
_____
_____
_____

When I am faced with racism, I react by
_____
_____
_____
_____
_____
_____

When I sense racism toward me, I will
_____
_____
_____
_____
_____
_____

Encouragement: You are the people (1 Peter 2:10).

It's a Setup | 12

Has someone ever been dishonest toward you with the intent to destroy your character? Maybe someone wanted you out of the way at your place of work. Maybe someone wanted the person you liked for themselves. There are evil people that work to set traps for you to fall into. Whatever the reason, being set-up can threaten your security and cause you to lose trust. Mark 12: 13: "Then they sent some of the Pharisees and Herodians to Him in order to trap Him in a statement." What this means is that *who would be able to trust Him?* Jesus understands what it is like to have crafty people set Him up to fail. Jesus was doing good for the people, but these wicked ones sought to stop Him by discrediting His teachings. If Jesus were caught in a lie or with some inaccurate statement, who would be able to trust Him? Take comfort that you have a Savior who understands. He understands because He has faced the same things you do, and He has overcome them all.

Prayer: Lord, some terrible people have done me wrong. Please help me to forgive them, and please give me the favor to make things right. Amen.

Journal: Bad Intentions; Perfect Results

When _____ set me up to fail, I felt _____
          (name)

_____

_____

_____

_____

_____

_____

When I feel like I am being set-up, I react by

_____

_____

_____

_____

_____

_____

When I think I am being set-up, I will

_____

_____

_____

_____

_____

_____

_____

Encouragement: God's got you (Romans 12:19).

It's about Your Stuff | 13

Have you ever had someone befriend you so they could take from you? Maybe you are a popular person, so someone hangs out with you to gain your popularity. Maybe you have achieved significant goals, or have material things. Some people do not want you, but they do want your stuff. Whatever the reason, being liked merely for your stuff can be a rude awakening. John 6:26: "Truly, truly, I say to you, you seek Me, not because you saw signs, but because you ate of the loaves and were filled." What this

they didn't want to learn means is that Jesus understands what it like for people to only want what He has to offer. The people only wanted Jesus' food. They called Jesus "Teacher" to fluff Him up, but they didn't want to learn from Him. All they wanted from Him was what He could give them. Take comfort that you have a Savior who understands. He understands because He has faced the same things you do, and He has overcome them all.

Prayer: I thought they really liked me for me, but I was wrong. Lord, help me to forgive, and help me find good relationships. Amen.

Journal: It's Only Stuff

When _____ took _____ from me, I felt _____
          (name)   (list taken)

_____

_____

_____

_____

_____

When it appears someone is going to take from me,

I react by _____

_____

_____

_____

_____

_____

When I think I am being stolen from, I will _____

_____

_____

_____

_____

_____

Encouragement: Provider (Philippians 4:19).

I Will, but I Will Not | 14

Have you ever had someone tell you that they would, but then they didn't? They say, "I will," but they will not. Maybe someone offered to help you. Maybe they promised to never leave you. Sometimes, people mean well, but cannot fulfill their promises. Many people have no intention of doing what they say. Whatever the reason, being given a promise only to be left without can make you feel taken. Matthew 26:33: "But Peter said to Him, 'Even though all may fall away because of You, I will never fall away.'" What this means is *unable to deliver on his promise* that Jesus understands what it is like to have His friend promise loyalty to Him, but later not follow through with the commitment. Peter fully intended to stay by Jesus' side to the bitter end. Peter was unable to deliver on his promise. It appeared that Peter's devotion was noble, but he only had his own interests in mind. Take comfort that you have a Savior who understands. He understands because He has faced the same things you do, and He has overcome them all.

Prayer: I thought they were true to their word. Lord, help me to be wise in my expectations. Amen.

Journal: Be Good to Your Word

When _____ told me they would _____ but
             (name)   (do what)

let me down, I felt _____

_____

_____

_____

_____

_____

_____

When someone tells me they will do a certain thing, but
they do not, I react by _____

_____

_____

_____

_____

_____

_____

When someone gives me their word, I will _____

_____

_____

_____

_____

_____

_____

Encouragement: Every single time, without fail (Numbers 23:19).

Threatened | 15

Have you ever had someone threaten to take your life? Maybe they could not bring themselves to take your life physically, but for sure, they have conspired it in their thoughts. Maybe it is that someone really has tried to kill you. If you are in the way of what someone wants, and they want it bad enough, you may become a danger in their mind. Whatever the reason, having your life threatened can be a scary proposition. Luke 4:29: "And they got up and drove Him (Jesus) out of the city, and led Him to the brow of the hill, in order to throw Him down the cliff." What this means is that Jesus understands what it is like to have His life threatened. Jesus was led out to be killed. The people did not like what He said, so they got mad and proceeded to throw Him off the edge of the cliff to His death. Take comfort that you have a Savior who understands. He understands because He has faced the same things you do, and He has overcome them all.

led out to be killed

Prayer: Lord, they have killed me in their mind. They wish me dead. Please protect me from wrong and help me to forgive them. If I have hurt them, please help me make it right. Amen.

Journal: Shaken but Not Stirred

When _____ told me they would _____ to me,

          (name)   (do what)

I felt _____

_____

_____

_____

_____

_____

When I feel I am in danger, I react by _____

_____

_____

_____

_____

_____

_____

When I am threatened, I will _____

_____

_____

_____

_____

_____

_____

Encouragement: Not moved (Psalm 16:8).

Poked Fun At | 16

Have you ever been ridiculed? Maybe you are shorter than everyone else. Maybe you are not as affluent as the rest of the group, or maybe you didn't get the punch line of the joke. This situation can challenge you to want to fight or embarrass you to run away and hide. This is especially true if it happens in front of people that you care about. Whatever the reason, being made fun of is horrible. Mathew 27:29: "...and then twisted together a crown of thorns and set it on his head. They belittled in front of the whole town put a staff in his right hand. Then they knelt in front of him and mocked him. 'Hail, king of the Jews!' they said." What this means is that Jesus understands what it is like to be ridiculed. Jesus was mocked as if He were a fake king. Jesus was taunted because the people did not understand who He truly was. Jesus was belittled in front of the whole town. Take comfort that you have a Savior who understands. He understands because He has faced the same things you do, and He has overcome them all.

Prayer: Lord, I don't like it when they make fun of me. Help me forgive them. Amen.

Journal: Not Funny

When _____ ridiculed me, I felt _____
        (name)

_____

_____

_____

_____

_____

_____

_____

When I am made fun of or laughed at, I react by

_____

_____

_____

_____

_____

_____

_____

When I am poked fun at, I will

_____

_____

_____

_____

_____

_____

_____

_____

Encouragement: Making fun: don't do it (Proverbs 19:29).

I'm Innocent | 17

Have you ever been accused of wrongdoing, but you were innocent? Maybe something came up missing, and you were to blame. Maybe a project at your place of work was late, and you were made out to be at fault. Any judgment is difficult, but more so when you know that you are not guilty. Whatever the reason, being wrongly charged for wrongdoing puts you on trial to prove yourself. Mark 15:14: "'Why? What crime has he committed?' asked Pilate." What this means is that Jesus understands what it is like to be innocent, but be charged as guilty. Jesus was publically and viciously accused of crimes He did not commit. Jesus was falsely accused of things that were not even crimes. Jesus understands what it is like to have His innocence portrayed as guilt. Take comfort that you have a Savior who understands. He understands because He has faced the same things you do, and He has overcome them all.

innocence portrayed as guilt

Prayer: Lord, I did not do what they have accused me of. Let my honesty be sufficient. Amen.

Journal: Truth Told

When _____ blamed me for something I did not do,

I felt _____ (name) _____

_____

_____

_____

_____

_____

_____

When I am falsely accused, I react by _____

_____

_____

_____

_____

_____

_____

When wrongful fault is put on me, I will _____

_____

_____

_____

_____

_____

_____

_____

Encouragement: No crooked paths (Proverbs 10:9).

Someone Took It | 18

Have you ever had something taken from you? Maybe someone you didn't know has stolen from you. On the other hand, maybe it was someone you knew and trusted. It is dreadful enough to have your things taken, but it is much worse when it is done by someone you trust. What would you think if you found out that your employer was skimming money from your paychecks? Whatever the reason, being stolen from hurts and leaves you feeling exposed. John 12:6: "Now he (Judas) said this because he was a thief, and as he had the money box, he used to pilfer (steal) what was put into it." What this means is that Jesus understands what it is like to have His possessions taken. Jesus trusted Judas with His money, but Judas took advantage of Him. Judas did not want the money for the poor, but rather he wanted it for himself. Jesus understands what it is like to be stolen from. Take comfort that you have a Savior who understands. He understands because He has faced the same things you do, and He has overcome them all.

Prayer: Lord, my stuff is gone. Help me to be okay without it, and help me to forgive them for taking it. Amen.

Journal: Returned

When _____ took from me, I felt _____

(name)

_____

_____

_____

_____

_____

_____

When someone tries to take what belongs to me, I react by

_____

_____

_____

_____

_____

_____

When my things are threatened, I will

_____

_____

_____

_____

_____

_____

_____

Encouragement: Pick up the pieces (Deuteronomy 30:3).

You're the One | 19

Have you ever been blamed for something that is not your fault? Maybe the faucet was not shut off completely, and it was found dripping. Maybe your friend made a mistake, and you were blamed for not telling them what to do. Maybe something was broken. You did not break it, but somehow it was your fault anyway. Many people desire a scapegoat for a crisis, so they blame. It was not them, so it had to be you. If you had done this, then that would not have happened. Whatever the reason, being held responsible without fault is unjust. John 11:32: "'Lord,' Martha said to Jesus, 'if you had been here, my brother would not have died.'" What this means is that Jesus understands what it is like to be blamed for things that were not His fault. Jesus was made out to be responsible for Lazarus's death. Lazarus became sick and passed away. It was not Jesus' fault that Martha's brother died, but He was blamed. Take comfort that you have a Savior who understands. He understands because He has faced the same things you do, and He has overcome them all.

He was blamed

Prayer: Lord, you know it was not my fault. Help me to forgive those who blamed me. Amen.

Journal: It's Not Mine

When _____ said it was my fault, I felt _____
     (name)

_____

_____

_____

_____

_____

_____

When someone tries to blame me, I react by _____

_____

_____

_____

_____

_____

_____

_____

When I am blamed for something, I will _____

_____

_____

_____

_____

_____

_____

_____

_____

Encouragement: Not to blame (1 Thessalonians 5:23).

Misunderstood | 20

Have you ever been misunderstood? Maybe you thought you were being clear, but they just did not catch what you were saying. It can be extremely frustrating when you try to explain, but your audience is unable to understand. You know they have misinterpreted you, and nothing you can say enlightens them. Whatever the reason, being misunderstood is irritating. Luke 2:50: "But they did not understand the statement which He had made to them." What this means is that Jesus understands what it is like to be misunderstood. Jesus spoke to His audience, but they did not relate to His words. In this particular case, Jesus was speaking with His parents. Jesus clearly explained His position, but His parents did not understand. Take comfort that you have a Savior who understands. He understands because He has faced the same things you do, and He has overcome them all.

Clearly Explained

Prayer: Lord, I get _____ when people don't understand me. Please help me to be more tolerant. Amen.

Journal: Who Gets Me?

When _____ did not understand what I was saying,

I felt _____ (name) _____

_____

_____

_____

_____

_____

_____

When I am not understood, I react by _____

_____

_____

_____

_____

_____

_____

When someone does not get what I am saying, I will _____

_____

_____

_____

_____

_____

_____

_____

_____

Encouragement: Even my thoughts (Psalm 139:2).

Turned His Back | 21

Has anyone ever turned their back on you? Maybe you were going through a trying time, and it felt like your friend was nowhere to be found. Maybe you did what was right, but the wrongdoers gained the upper hand. When this happens, it looks like even God had turned His back on you. You know that God doesn't turn away from you. Many times, we are just mad because things did not go our way. Whatever the reason, the feeling that a friend, or even God Himself has turned away from

abandoned   you can cause you to feel abandoned. Matthew 27:46: "MY GOD, MY GOD, WHY HAVE YOU FORSAKEN ME?" What this means is that Jesus understands what it is like to be abandoned.

Not only did Jesus experience a friend that turned away from Him, God turned His back on Him. God had to turn away from Him because Jesus took on our sin. Father God abandoned Jesus at the Cross. Take comfort that you have a Savior who understands. He understands because He has faced the same things you do, and He has overcome them all.

Prayer: Lord, it hurts me that those I have put my hope in have turned away from me, and I am sorry for accusing You of leaving me. Help me to forgive those who have left me, and know that You will never leave me alone. Amen.

Journal: Absent When Needed

When _____ turned their back on me, I felt _____
           (name)

_____

_____

_____

_____

_____

_____

When someone leaves me, I react by _____

_____

_____

_____

_____

_____

_____

When someone turns away from me, I will _____

_____

_____

_____

_____

_____

_____

_____

Encouragement: Never leave (Hebrews 13:5).

Guilty Goes Free | 22

Have you ever been made out to be guilty and had to watch the one who was really at fault go free? Maybe a driver zoomed past you speeding, and the officer stopped you. Maybe someone at your place of work left the equipment running, and you were made out to be responsible. Whatever the reason, being without guilt and having to watch the guilty go free can make you feel cheated. Matthew 27:16: "Whom do you want me to release for you? Barabbas, or Jesus..." What this means is sentenced to that Jesus understands what it is like to watch the death guilty go free. Jesus was innocent, yet He had to watch the crook, Barabbas, go free. Yes, that day, Barabbas, who was previously convicted of crimes, went away a free man. Meanwhile, Jesus was sentenced to death. Take comfort that you have a Savior who understands. He understands because He has faced the same things you do, and He has overcome them all.

Prayer: Lord, You see everything, and You know what happened. Help me to be okay with what You have allowed, and I know You will bring justice. Amen.

Journal: Guilt to Freedom

When _____ was guilty and I took the blame, I felt
        (name)

_____

_____

_____

_____

_____

_____

When I am innocent but said to be guilty, I react by

_____

_____

_____

_____

_____

_____

When I am made out to be in the wrong, I will

_____

_____

_____

_____

_____

_____

_____

Encouragement: Free indeed (John 8:36).

Disloyalty | 23

Have you ever been betrayed? Maybe someone wanted to get ahead for themselves, so they were disloyal to you. Maybe a friend ratted you out, and you had to pay the price because they did. Good relationships are tremendously difficult to come by, so when you have a special relationship, you do everything you can to protect it. This is all wasted when someone betrays you. Whatever the reason, being betrayed can make it difficult to trust again. Matthew 26:48: "Now he (Judas) *betrayed by someone close* who was betraying Him gave them a sign, saying, 'Whomever I kiss, He is the one; seize Him.'" What this means is that Jesus understands what it means to be betrayed by someone close. Judas kissed Jesus, yet Jesus called Judas, "friend." Jesus was then arrested and taken away. Take comfort that you have a Savior who understands. He understands because He has faced the same things you do, and He has overcome them all.

Prayer: Lord, they gave me up, and I am upset about it. Help me to forgive them, and let Your favor be with me. Amen.

Journal: Still Here

When _____ betrayed me, I felt _____
            (name)

_____

_____

_____

_____

_____

_____

When someone is disloyal to me, I react by _____

_____

_____

_____

_____

_____

_____

When I am handed over to those who are against me, I will _____

_____

_____

_____

_____

_____

_____

_____

Encouragement: Everyone but You (Psalm 27:10).

Suffering of Others | 24

Have you ever had to watch someone suffer? Maybe it was a loved one who became seriously ill. Maybe it was that a good friend lost someone dear to them. Maybe those you know lost everything in a violent storm. Sometimes, you might be able to fix the situation, but other times, you may not. Whatever the reason, having to watch those you care about suffer can make you feel powerless. John 19:25: "Near the cross of Jesus stood his mother, his mother's sister, Mary the wife of Clopas, and Mary Magdalene." What this means is that Jesus looked down at His family and friends as they suffered His death. In following verses, Jesus tries to refocus His mom to her son, and her son to His mom. Jesus understands what it is like to watch His loved ones suffer while only being able to offer words as comfort to them. Take comfort that you have a Savior who understands. He understands because He has faced the same things you do, and He has overcome them all.

watch His loved ones suffer

Prayer: Lord, You know it is painful to watch the ones you love suffering. Please help me to be strong and be there for those who need me. Amen.

Journal: How Can I Help?

When I watched _____ suffering, I felt _____

                          (name)

_____

_____

_____

_____

_____

_____

When I see someone suffering, I react by

_____

_____

_____

_____

_____

_____

When someone is undergoing a struggle, I will

_____

_____

_____

_____

_____

_____

_____

Encouragement: Get comfort; give comfort (2 Corinthians 1:3).

What's the Answer? | 25

Have you ever needed an answer? Maybe you have been questioned, but you are not sure how to answer. Maybe you needed the answers during an important test. Maybe there is no apparent answer, and you are trapped in a no-win situation. Whatever the reason, being forced to answer when you have no answer can cause you to panic. John 8:6-7: "But Jesus stooped down and with His finger wrote on the ground. But when they persisted in asking Him, He straightened up, and said to them..." What this means is that Jesus understands what it is like to be without an answer. Jesus was challenged with a difficult question that seemed to have no right answer. Jesus took time to bend down and write on the ground. Perhaps He was buying time until He could find an exacting answer. The people continued to badger Him, so Jesus had to respond, Eventually, His answer did come. Take comfort that you have a Savior who understands. He understands because He has faced the same things you do, and He has overcome them all.

no right answer

Prayer: Lord, it is unnerving when I don't have the answer. Please help me to remember that You are always there for me, and You will give me an answer in due time. Amen.

Journal: What to Say?

When _____ , and I didn't have an answer, I felt
         (what happened)

_____

_____

_____

_____

_____

_____

_____

When I don't have an answer to a problem, I react by _____

_____

_____

_____

_____

_____

_____

_____

When I don't have the answer, I will _____

_____

_____

_____

_____

_____

_____

_____

_____

Encouragement: You have the answer (Matthew 10:19-20).

Not My Problem | 26

Have you ever been asked to fix a problem that has nothing to do with you? Maybe you were a guest at someone's party, and at the last minute, you were asked to help the host of the party. Maybe a child was acting out, but they were not your child. This can put you on the spot to respond. When something is a crisis for another person, they can dump it off on you even though it is not your problem. Whatever the reason, being required to make a quick decision about something that someone

asked to fix a problem

else is in charge of can make you feel unsure of yourself. John 2:4: "And Jesus said to her, 'Woman (referring to His mom), what does that have to do with us?'" What this means is that Jesus understands what it is like to be expected to fix someone else's problem. Jesus was asked to fix a problem that had nothing to do with Him. He was a guest at the party, along with His mom. Mom decided to volunteer Jesus to fix the problem that was the responsibility of the party's host. Thanks, Mom. Take comfort that you have a Savior who understands. He understands because He has faced the same things you do, and He has overcome them all.

Prayer: Lord, You know it was not my problem. Please give me wisdom, and like Jesus, help me to be more giving when it is right to do so. Amen.

Journal: Maybe I Can Help

When _____ expected me to fix a problem I was not

_____(name)_____

responsible for, I felt _____

_____

_____

_____

_____

_____

_____

When I have to fix someone else's problems, I react by

_____

_____

_____

_____

_____

_____

_____

When I am asked to fix an issue that is not mine, I will

_____

_____

_____

_____

_____

_____

_____

Encouragement: Not His problem, but He fixed it (Ephesians 2:5).

Malicious Dislike | 27

Have you ever been hated—not just a dislike, but dislike with malicious intent? They intend to hurt you and even take you out. Maybe you are not like them. Maybe you have a life they are jealous of. Maybe you did something that hurt them; maybe they hate you without cause. If you are hated, and you can defend yourself, you spend a lifetime watching your back, but if you cannot defend yourself you are continually afraid of what might become. Whatever the reason, being hated is no good. John 15:18: "If the world hates you, you know that it has hated Me before it hated you." What this means is that Jesus understands what it is like to be despised. Jesus was hated before you were hated. Jesus was misunderstood by His own people before He was born. Jesus came to help the world, but the world would not and still does not understand Him. Just like you, He is not accepted by those who have darkened hearts. Jesus was not like the world, so the world hated Him. Take comfort that you have a Savior who understands. He understands because He has faced the same things you do, and He has overcome them all.

misunderstood by His own people

Prayer: Lord, You know that I am intensely disliked. You know what this feels like. Please help me to overcome. Amen.

Journal: Despicable Me

When _____ expressed their hatred toward me, I felt
(name)

_____

_____

_____

_____

_____

_____

_____

When I am disliked, I react by _____

_____

_____

_____

_____

_____

_____

When I am not liked, I will _____

_____

_____

_____

_____

_____

_____

Encouragement: World loved (John 3:16).

Flattered | 28

Have you ever been flattered by someone? You may not have realized it then, but the smooth comments were intended to draw you in to the lair of the one deceiving you. Maybe you have held a key position within a group or organization, and how well you were praised by someone who wanted to use your position for their benefit. Flattery is never given to promote you, but is always for the one delivering the amazing tribute. Whatever the reason, falling for flattery can make you feel used. Luke 20:21: "So the spies questioned him: "Teacher, we know that you speak and teach what is right, and that you do not show partiality but teach the way of God in accordance with the truth." What this means is that Jesus understands what it is like to be flattered. Jesus was praised by the spies, but they had no good intentions. These spies were sent to Jesus to catch Him in some fault statement. It is for sure that they put on a good show for Jesus, but they were only there to harm Him. Take comfort that you have a Savior who understands. He understands because He has faced the same things you do, and He has overcome them all.

praised by the spies

Prayer: Lord, I wanted to believe what _____ said about me, but now I know it was only to deceive me. Please help me to forgive _____, and to be confident in myself and not fall for smooth talk . Amen.

Journal: Redeemed Offender

When _____ flattered me to get what they wanted,
I felt _____(name)_____

_____

_____

_____

_____

_____

When I am flattered, I react by _____

_____

_____

_____

_____

_____

When someone complements me, I will _____

_____

_____

_____

_____

_____

_____

_____

Encouragement: Test it out first (1 John 4:1)

I Don't Owe That | 29

Have you ever had to pay for something that you did not owe? Maybe you were once married and are now divorced, and your ex-spouse left you with debt that was not caused by you. Maybe someone you know was given the "Friends and Family" discount, but you were denied the same benefit. Maybe you were required to pay for yourself, but others were not. Whatever the reason, being obligated to pay for something that is not your responsibility can be upsetting. Matthew 17:25-26: "Jesus spoke to him first, saying, 'What do you think, Simon? From whom do the kings of the earth collect customs or poll-tax, from their sons or from strangers?' When Peter said, 'From strangers,' Jesus said to him, 'Then the sons are exempt.'" What this means is that Jesus understands what it is like to be demanded of to pay something He did not owe. Jesus was a "Friends and Family," and, therefore, by His rights, should be excused from paying the tax. However, He was asked to pay a tax as if He were a foreigner. How did this make Him look in front of His friends and others? Jesus took the offense and paid what He did not owe, so He could have what was best for Him and His friends. Take comfort that you have a Savior who understands. He understands because He has faced the same things you do, and He has overcome them all.

paid what He did not owe

Prayer: Lord, You know that I should not have had to pay for _____. I forgive. If it is in Your heart, please provide for me like You did for Jesus. Amen.

Journal: I Can Pay

When _____, I was expected to pay what I didn't

(what happened)

owe, and I felt _____

_____

_____

_____

_____

_____

_____

When I am demanded to pay what I don't owe, I react by _____

_____

_____

_____

_____

_____

_____

When I face having to pay what I do not owe, I will _____

_____

_____

_____

_____

_____

_____

_____

Encouragement: Even the small is given (Matthew 17:27).

Not Welcome Here | 30

Have you ever been asked to leave because the people did not want you around? Maybe you were trying to do good, but that exposed what they were really up to. Maybe they were with a certain crowd, and they felt you did not fit in. Maybe it is fine that you hang out, but when "they" show up, you are no longer welcome? It is not that you are doing something wrong, but it is clearly because of who you are. Whatever the reason, being unwanted is an awful experience. Matthew 8:34: "And behold, the whole city came out to meet Jesus; and when they saw Him, they implored Him to leave their region." What this means is that Jesus understands what it is like to not be welcome. Jesus was not wanted. Jesus was doing some amazing things for the people, but the people did not want Him to be in their town. Take comfort that you have a Savior who understands. He understands because He has faced the same things you do, and He has overcome them all.

the people did not want Him

Prayer: Lord, You know what it is like to not be received by others. I know that I am always welcome to be with You. Come be with me. Amen.

Journal: Not You!

When _____ did not welcome me, I felt _____
            (name)
_____
_____
_____
_____
_____
_____
_____

When I am not received, I react by _____
_____
_____
_____
_____
_____
_____

When I am not welcomed, I will _____
_____
_____
_____
_____
_____
_____
_____

Encouragement: Invited in (Romans 15:7).

Discarded | 31

Have you ever been rejected, not just by anyone, but by your own family or friends? If your own blood rejects you, you have been rejected by your closest inner circle. The saying is that blood is thicker than water. It is one thing to be rejected by those who are not expected to love you, but it is another to be rejected by those who are supposed to be the strongest and most important to you. Maybe you have been thrown to the side by a sibling or even your parents. Whatever the reason, being rejected is horrible. John 1:11: "He came to His own, and those who were His own did not receive Him." What this means is that Jesus understands what it is like to be shunned. Jesus was rejected by His own people. These people knew Him personally. It might be understandable that Jesus could be rejected by those who did not know Him, but these were His own blood, His own people, His family. Take comfort that you have a Savior who understands. He understands because He has faced the same things you do, and He has overcome them all.

rejected by His own people

Prayer: Lord, I have been pushed aside by those who were supposed to love me. I thank You that You always love me. If it is possible, allow this brokenness to be put back together. Amen.

Journal: Treasure Not Trash

When _____ rejected me, I felt _____
           (name)
_____
_____
_____
_____
_____
_____
_____

When I am not wanted, I react by _____
_____
_____
_____
_____
_____
_____
_____

When I am not received, I will _____
_____
_____
_____
_____
_____
_____
_____
_____

Encouragement: Never forgotten (Isaiah 49:15).

Please Pray | 32

Have you ever needed someone to pray for you? Maybe you were going through a hard time, and you needed someone to stand with you. Maybe you wanted prayer for direction in a matter. Have you ever asked the person if they had prayed, and they could not answer you? This can make you feel like what you are going through is not important, and the person who is supposed to pray for you is just not there for you. Whatever the reason, not being supported in a time of need can leave you feeling disappointed. Matthew 26:38: "Then He said to them, 'My soul is deeply grieved, to the point of death; remain here and keep watch with Me.'" What this means is that Jesus understands what it is like to ask for prayer, yet receive none. Jesus asked His friends to stay with Him and pray with Him while He asked for direction. The phrase "keep watch" means to watch out in a protective way, but Jesus only returned to find His friends sleeping when He needed them most. All He asked them to do was pray for Him. Take comfort that you have a Savior who understands. He understands because He has faced the same things you do, and He has overcome them all.

Prayer: Lord, I asked _____ to pray for me, to look out for me, and I was let down. I thank You that You always hear my prayers. Amen.

Journal: Always Praying

When I asked _____, and they did not pray for me,
                  (name)
I felt

_____

_____

_____

_____

_____

_____

When I want help, but none comes, I react by

_____

_____

_____

_____

_____

_____

When I need prayer and support, I will

_____

_____

_____

_____

_____

_____

_____

Encouragement: Ultimate prayer warrior (Romans 8:34).

The Wrong Crowd | 33

Have you ever been seen with people that others didn't think you should be with? You strive to be inclusive of those who are less than desirable, but in some circles, it is forbidden to be seen with such people. Maybe you have been seen talking with a working girl, or a bum under a bridge. When you are found with the undesirable, you may be treated as dirty or doing something wrong. Whatever the reason, being shunned for being accepting of the unwanted can cause you to become angry and reject your *criticized for reaching out* accusers. Matthew 9:10-11: "While Jesus was having dinner at Matthew's house, many tax collectors and sinners came and ate with him and his disciples. When the Pharisees saw this, they asked his disciples, 'Why does your teacher eat with tax collectors and sinners?'" What this means is that Jesus understands what it is like to be criticized for reaching out to the lost. Jesus was having dinner with His new disciple Matthew, who was a former tax collector. Matthew's worldly friends and business colleagues stopped by, and Jesus was criticized, by the religious leaders, for not denouncing them. Take comfort that you have a Savior who understands. He understands because He has faced the same things you do, and He has overcome them all.

Prayer: Lord, I want to be accommodating of all people. Even if I don't agree with them, I want to be able to offer them You. Please give me the strength when I am charged with being kind to the undesirable. Amen.

Journal: Have Good; Do Good

When _____ did not approve of who I was talking to,

I felt _____ (name) _____

_____

_____

_____

_____

_____

_____

When who I speak to is disapproved of, I react by _____

_____

_____

_____

_____

_____

_____

When I am said to be relating to those who are unapproved of,

I will _____

_____

_____

_____

_____

_____

_____

_____

Encouragement: Do what you can (1 John 3:17).

Do as I Say | 34

Have you ever been questioned for doing or not doing what others expected you to do or not do? Maybe there were those who signed up to participate in some type of activity, but you did not want to. Maybe there was a great cause, and it was assumed that you would participate as the others were doing. Maybe a group of people decide to go out and feed the hungry. There is no arguing that this is noble act, but this is not grounds for criticizing you for not joining them. Whatever the reason, this pressure can cause you to question yourself and possibly have feelings of guilt. Mark 2:18: "Now John's disciples and the Pharisees were fasting. Some people came and asked Jesus, 'How is it that John's disciples and the disciples of the Pharisees are fasting, but yours are not?'" What this means is that Jesus understands what it is like to be criticized for not doing what others thought He should be doing. Jesus agreed that fasting is proper at the appropriate time. He gave His position on the matter, which provided a good reason for why His disciples were not fasting. Even with this, they criticized Him. Take comfort that you have a Savior who understands. He understands because He has faced the same things you do, and He has overcome them all.

Prayer: Lord, I have many telling me what I should and should not do. I want to grow and gain understanding. Please help me to have wisdom to know what I should do and when. Amen.

Journal: To Do or Not to Do?

When _____ expected me to do because others are
_____ (name) _____

doing, I felt _____

_____

_____

_____

_____

_____

_____

When I am told what to do, I react by _____

_____

_____

_____

_____

_____

_____

When I am given direction that I do not agree with, I will ___

_____

_____

_____

_____

_____

_____

Encouragement: The best teacher (John 14:26).

Fake Friend | 35

Have you ever had a friend that turned out to be fake? Trust must be earned over time. When trust is tested, it is proven or disproven. Maybe you had a friend that you entrusted with things that were private and deeply important to you. Maybe you let someone borrow an item that was important to you, and they broke it. Maybe you confided in someone, and they told others about what you had said to them. This breach of trust worsens when you find out that they were only out for themselves. It was their intention to use you for their benefit. Whatever the reason, finding out that a friend is fake is heartbreaking and can make it difficult to trust again. Luke 22:48: "But Jesus said to him, 'Judas, are you betraying the Son of Man with a kiss?'" What this means is that Jesus understands what it is like to have a friend that turns out to be fake. Judas ministered with Jesus for some time, and Jesus appointed Judas to manage the finances for Him and His disciples. In the end, Judas chose to pursue money and power over his loyalty to Jesus. Judas betrayed Jesus by turning Him over to His captors. Take comfort that you have a Savior who understands. He understands because He has faced the same things you do, and He has overcome them all.

Prayer: Lord, I thought they were my friends. Like You, I trusted them, but they deceived me. Please help me to forgive them so that I can trust again. Amen.

Journal: I Can Have a True Friend

When _____ turned out to be a fake friend, I felt
_____(name)_____

_____

_____

_____

_____

_____

_____

_____

When people are counterfeit, I react by _____

_____

_____

_____

_____

_____

_____

When I find that someone is being phony, I will _____

_____

_____

_____

_____

_____

_____

_____

_____

Encouragement: They do exist (Proverbs 17:17).

Labeled | 36

Have you ever been stereotyped? You were labeled before you even spoke. Maybe you were raised on a farm, and by default, you were presumed to be simple-minded. Maybe you are from a certain neighborhood, and therefore, are considered to be a dangerous person. Maybe you are from a different school, church, or group than those who are laying judgment. You are shut down before you get a chance to show the true you. Whatever the reason, being labeled is an unfounded charge, and this can cause you to feel unfairly treated. John 4:9: "The Samaritan woman said to him, 'You are a Jew and I am a Samaritan woman. How can you ask me for a drink?' (For Jews do not associate with Samaritans.)" What this means is that Jesus understands what it is like to be labeled. Jesus was a Jew, but He was no typical Jew. In verse 10, Jesus let her know that she did not know Him, and then He proceeded to show her a love that she had never experienced from anyone and much less from a Jew. Take comfort that you have a Savior who understands. He understands because He has faced the same things you do, and He has overcome them all.

a love that she had never experienced

Prayer: Lord, I am who I am because You created me. Help me to be tolerant of those who judge me before they know me. Give me wisdom and strength to be who I am. Amen.

Journal: It's Just Me

When _____ wrongly labeled me, I felt
          (name)

_____

_____

_____

_____

_____

_____

When I am said to be something I am not, I react by

_____

_____

_____

_____

_____

_____

When I am stereotyped, I will

_____

_____

_____

_____

_____

_____

_____

Encouragement: Ask Him; He made me (Ephesians 2:10).

Jealous | 37

Has anyone ever been jealous of you? Maybe you have received a raise, reward, or promotion that others thought should have gone to them. Maybe you have built relationships that others want for themselves. Jealousy can cause people to take unmerited action. Maybe their jealousy caused them to place false complaints about you or damage things that belong to you. Whatever the reason, being the object of others' jealousy creates an uneasy tone. John 3:25-26: "Therefore there arose a discussion (argument) on the part of John's disciples with a Jew about purification. And they came to John and said to him, 'Rabbi, He (Jesus) who was with you beyond the Jordan, to whom you have testified, behold, He is baptizing and ALL are coming to Him.'" What this means is that Jesus understands what it is like for people to be envious of Him. Jesus' success provoked jealousy in the hearts of John's followers. Jesus and John were fond of each other as expressed by the testimony of both about each other, but John's disciples did not like someone else encroaching on their territory. Take comfort that you have a Savior who understands. He understands because He has faced the same things you do, and He has overcome them all.

success provoked jealousy

Prayer: Lord, I know that there are those who are jealous of me. I don't want them to envy me. Please help me to be patient with those who are jealous of me. Amen.

Journal: No Envy

When _____ was jealous of me, I felt _____
                    (name)

_____

_____

_____

_____

_____

_____

When someone is envious of me, I react by _____

_____

_____

_____

_____

_____

When someone is jealousy of me, I will _____

_____

_____

_____

_____

_____

_____

Encouragement: Examine and take pride (Galatians 6:4).

Don't Tell Me That | 38

Have you ever had to tell someone something they did not want to hear? Maybe you had to tell someone difficult news. Maybe you noticed that a person was going down a wrong path in their life, and that person would find your advice difficult or impossible to accept. Move too fast and you could do more harm than good, yet in contrast, it is much easier to do nothing. The truth will sting, so it is best told in love. Do you love people more than your own image? Whatever the reason, being the messenger with difficult news is not easy. Mark 10:21: "Looking at him (rich young ruler), Jesus felt a love for him and said to him, 'One thing you lack: go and sell all you possess and give to the poor, and you will have treasure in heaven; and come, follow Me.' But at these words he was saddened, and he went away grieving, for he was one who owned much property." What this means is that Jesus understands what it is like to have to give an unpopular answer. Jesus liked the young man, and He wanted the best for him. Jesus could have gone on His way, but He chose to tell the man what was best for him. The young man was crushed by Jesus' words. In other words, Jesus hurt his feelings, and then Jesus had to watch him walk away broken. Take comfort that you have a Savior who understands. He understands because He has faced the same things you do, and He has overcome them all.

watch him walk away broken

Prayer: Lord, even though I know it is best, it is hard for me to break difficult news to those I care about. Help me to see that what You ask me to do is good. Please give me the words that You would say to them. Amen.

Journal: I Just Can't Say It

When I had to confront _____, I felt _____

            (name)

_____

_____

_____

_____

_____

_____

When I must confront someone, I react by _____

_____

_____

_____

_____

_____

When I must confront someone, I will _____

_____

_____

_____

_____

_____

_____

_____

Encouragement: It is better to save a soul (James 5:19-20).

Stand Up | 39

Have you ever had to stand up for what is right? Maybe there have been those who were left out, and you spoke up on their behalf. Maybe you pitched in to help those who are hungry. Maybe you encouraged someone whose dreams had been crushed. Maybe you have seen someone being mistreated, and you had the backbone to step in. Standing up can sometimes have the appearance of rebellion, but there is no greater sign of integrity than to stand up for what is right. Whatever the reason, standing up for what is right can be unpopular, and, initially, you may find yourself standing alone. Mark 11:17: "And He began to teach and say to them, 'Is it not written, 'MY HOUSE SHALL BE CALLED A HOUSE OF PRAYER FOR ALL THE NATIONS '? But you have made it a ROBBERS' DEN.'" What this means is that Jesus understands what it is like to stand up for what is right. Jesus would not stand for the mistreatment of the church. How would the world see Him if His house was allowed to be a place for thieves? Jesus whipped them and threw out the merchant robbers. This astonished the people and made Jesus extremely unpopular with the temple leadership. Take comfort that you have a Savior who understands. He understands because He has faced the same things you do, and He has overcome them all.

Prayer: Lord, if I see something that is not right in Your eyes, help me to be strong and stand up. Amen.

Journal: It's Right

When I faced standing up for _____ , I felt _____
  (what)

_____

_____

_____

_____

_____

_____

When I must defend what is right, I react by _____

_____

_____

_____

_____

_____

When what is right is mistreated, I will _____

_____

_____

_____

_____

_____

_____

Encouragement: Not for nothing (1 Corinthians 15:58, Proverbs 31:9).

Who's the Boss? | 40

Have you ever had your authority questioned? Maybe your abilities have been challenged at your work or as the leader of a team. Maybe you have had children, and they thought they were the parent. If you are the authority on anything, you must expect to be challenged. The proving of your authority brings validation to your title. Whatever the reason, having your authority questioned can make you defensive, yet it is your response to the challenge that is particularly important. Mark 11:28: "...and (the synagogue leaders) began saying to Him, 'By what authority are You doing these things, or who gave You this authority to do these things?'" What this means is that Jesus understands what it is like to have His authority questioned. Jesus' authority was challenged, because Jesus was doing things that those who were opposing Him were supposed to be doing, and they did not like it. Remember, there was no New Testament Bible then, so the people of Jesus' day did not know Him as the Son of God like you and I do. They were the authority, and to them, Jesus was just another man. How dare Jesus do things they could not do! Take comfort that you have a Savior who understands. He understands because He has faced the same things you do, and He has overcome them all.

authority was challenged

Prayer: Lord, I thank You for the abilities that I have. When I am tested, please help me to know who I am. Amen.

Journal: Authority Given

When _____ questioned my authority, I felt _____
        (name)

_____

_____

_____

_____

_____

_____

_____

When my authority is challenged, I react by _____

_____

_____

_____

_____

_____

_____

When my authority is disputed, I will _____

_____

_____

_____

_____

_____

_____

_____

_____

Encouragement: It won't hurt you (Luke 10:19).

Forbidden | 41

Have you ever had someone try to stop you from doing something you enjoy? Maybe you love to take nature walks, but due to some issue, the trails were closed. Maybe you want to see someone who is sick, but you are unable to because of someone else's decision. Maybe you love to play or watch sports, but the event was rained out. Doing what you love takes precious time, and it is hard when this time is taken away. Whatever the reason, not being able to do something you love can be disappointing. Mark 10:13: "And they were bringing children to Him so that He might touch them; but the disciples rebuked them." What this means is that Jesus understands what it is like to be blocked from something He loved to do. The disciples tried to prevent the children from coming to Jesus. For sure, the disciples did not mean harm to the kids, but rather they were looking out for what they thought was in Jesus' best interests. Jesus loved the little children, and He wanted to take time with them. Remember, Jesus taught the people to be like children so that they could enjoy heaven's goodness. Take comfort that you have a Savior who understands. He understands because He has faced the same things you do, and He has overcome them all.

Prayer: Lord, help me accept when the time is not right for me to do the things I love. Also, give me strength to overcome obstacles to doing the things I love. Amen.

Journal: Yes I Can

When _____ tried to stop me from _____ ,
I felt _____ (name) _____ (what)

_____

_____

_____

_____

_____

When I am prevented from doing what I love, I react by

_____

_____

_____

_____

When something tries to take away the things I love to do,
I will

_____

_____

_____

_____

_____

Encouragement: Well-trained (Psalm 144:1).

What's the Hold-Up? 42

Have you ever wanted time to pass by quickly? Maybe you had to take a medical test, and you wanted the results to come back pronto. Maybe when you were in school, you were eager to graduate. Maybe you were in a hurry to get married. Maybe you have been on a long trip, and it was taking forever. Whatever the reason, wanting time to move along can make your situation feel like it is going to last for all eternity. Mark 14:35: "And He (Jesus) went a little beyond them, and fell to the ground and began to pray that if it were possible, the hour might pass Him by." What this means is that Jesus understands what it is like to have to wait until the appointed time had come. Jesus was ready to move on from His situation. The pressure He was under was immense, so He was asking for any possible way to make time go faster. In the scope of His whole life, this was a short period of time, but it must have felt like it would last forever. Take comfort that you have a Savior who understands. He understands because He has faced the same things you do, and He has overcome them all.

ready to move on

Prayer: Lord, sometimes I am impatient. Many times, I become agitated over nothing, but sometimes my frustrations are justified. Please help me to see Your will for my life. Amen.

Journal: I Will Make It

When I had to wait because of _____ , I felt

(situation)

_____

_____

_____

_____

_____

_____

When tough situations drag on, I react by _____

_____

_____

_____

_____

_____

_____

When I face delays, I will _____

_____

_____

_____

_____

_____

_____

_____

Encouragement: Protected by peace (Philippians 4:7).

Gone Shopping | 43

Have you ever had to buy groceries? For sure, you have bought groceries for you and your family, but what about for a large gathering? Maybe it's not the money, but you don't like to grocery shop. Maybe you have been in charge of a large meal like for a wedding or a birthday. It can be a challenge to purchase everything that is needed, so maybe buying groceries is a major ordeal for you. Food and household supplies are required to live and are also necessary for a great party. Whatever the reason, buying groceries can be stressful. John 6:5: "Therefore Jesus, lifting up His eyes and seeing that a large crowd was coming to Him, said to Philip, 'Where are we to buy bread, so that these may eat?'" What this means is that Jesus understands what it is like to have to provide food for a large crowd. Jesus and His disciples had money to buy groceries for the crowd, however in this passage of Scripture, Jesus performed such a miraculous work that it is easy to overlook the fact that He was able and offered to buy food for the people. Jesus wanted the people to eat, and it was His pleasure to feed them. Take comfort that you have a Savior who understands. He understands because He has faced the same things you do, and He has overcome them all.

Prayer: Lord, You know the needs of my family and guests. You know that I love them. Please help me to always be able to provide for them, and also be kind to those who come into my home. Amen.

Journal: Provision

When _____ and I had to provide the food, I felt _____

_____

_____

_____

_____

_____

_____

_____

When the situation is difficult and I am responsible to
provide, I react by _____

_____

_____

_____

_____

_____

When I am unsure how I will provide, I will _____

_____

_____

_____

_____

_____

_____

Encouragement: More valuable than birds (Luke 12:24).

Transportation | 44

Have you ever been without a way to get to where you needed to go? Maybe your car was at the mechanic's shop. Maybe you didn't have a car. It is much more convenient to have your own ride. Depending on someone else for transportation means that you will have to fit in with their schedule, or worse, that you are unable to find a way to where you need to be. Whatever the reason, it can be awkward having no means of transportation.

needed transportation

Matthew 21:2: "...saying to them, 'Go into the village opposite you, and immediately you will find a donkey tied there and a colt with her; untie them and bring them to Me.'" What this means is that Jesus understand what it is like to be without a way to go where He needed to go. Jesus needed transportation. Jesus requested to borrow someone else's donkey, so He could use the donkey to ride into the town of Jerusalem. Take comfort that you have a Savior who understands. He understands because He has faced the same things you do, and He has overcome them all.

Prayer: Lord, if I am ever in need of a ride, please help me to be humble. Also, if someone needs a ride, let me remember to be kind. Amen.

Journal: I'll Get There

When I needed to go _____ and I had no way, I felt
                                       (where)

_____

_____

_____

_____

_____

_____

When I am stranded or without transportation, I react by

_____

_____

_____

_____

_____

_____

When I am in need of transportation, I will

_____

_____

_____

_____

_____

_____

_____

Encouragement: I can walk (John 5:8).

Missing | 45

Have others ever wondered where you were? Maybe you were at a friend's house, and your family or parents did not know where you were. Maybe you were out on a date, and it became past the time you were supposed to be home. When those who were looking for you find you, their fear turns into anger. Most likely, you were scolded. Whatever the reason, causing those you love this trouble can make you feel bad. Luke 2:48: "When they (His parents) saw Him, they were astonished; and His *parents were* mother said to Him, 'Son, why have You treated *responsible* us this way? Behold, Your father and I have been *for Him* anxiously looking for You.'" What this means is that Jesus understands what it is like to have His parents look for Him. Jesus was a child, and His parents were responsible for Him. When they could not find Him, they looked everywhere for Him. You know His Mom was not happy when she brought "your father" into the conversation. Take comfort that you have a Savior who understands. He understands because He has faced the same things you do, and He has overcome them all.

Prayer: Lord, I have been missed by my loved ones or those who care about me. Please help me to be considerate of their feelings. Amen.

Journal: I'll Be Back

When _____ , _____ became anxious,
        (what happened)   (name)

and I felt _____

_____

_____

_____

_____

When I am expected to be somewhere but I am not, I react by

_____

_____

_____

_____

_____

When someone worries about where I am, I will

_____

_____

_____

_____

_____

_____

_____

Encouragement: You'll find Him (Proverbs 8:17).

Trickery | 46

Have you ever been tricked? Maybe you have had a group of people who didn't like you very much, and they planned together how they could discredit you. Maybe your success at work, school, or in your community has made some people jealous. Their jealousy turned to anger, so they plotted together to damage your reputation. In some ways, it is better when they don't like you to your face rather than behind your back. Whatever the reason, being the target of a hateful scheme can **they wanted** be upsetting. Matthew 12:14: "But the Pharisees **to ruin Him** went out and conspired against Him, as to how they might destroy Him." What this means is that Jesus understands what it is like to have someone try to deceive Him. Jesus was the target of a hate crime. He understands what it is like to have extremely powerful people plot evil against Him. They didn't want to scare Him; they wanted to ruin Him. Jesus was helping many people, and the community leaders did not take kindly to His growing popularity. In secret, they planned to wipe Him out, and they finally found success when they murdered Him. Take comfort that you have a Savior who understands. He understands because He has faced the same things you do, and He has overcome them all.

Prayer: Lord, check my heart to make sure I do not have hate toward anyone. If I do, please take this out of my heart. If I am hated, remind me that You love me and will protect me. Amen.

Journal: I Need a Light

When _____ devised a plan to hurt my reputation,

I felt   *(name)*

_____

_____

_____

_____

_____

_____

When my reputation is at stake, I react by

_____

_____

_____

_____

_____

_____

When someone comes against my reputation, I will

_____

_____

_____

_____

_____

_____

_____

Encouragement: Daylight is coming (Luke 12:3).

Anonymous BFF | 47

Have you ever had a close friend who acted like they didn't know you? Maybe it was a friend that you grew up with. One day, the cool crowd arrived, and all of a sudden, you were forgotten. Maybe there was some trouble brewing, and your friend disassociated from you. Your BFF (best friend FOREVER)—how could a good friend turn away from you now? Whatever the reason, if a friend turns you away, the shock quickly turns to heartbreak. Luke 22:57: "But he (Peter) denied it, saying, 'Woman, I do not know Him.'" What this means is that Jesus understands what it is like to have someone claim to be a friend when no one is looking. One of Jesus' closest friends acted like he never knew Him. Jesus had put His heart into Peter, yet when trouble came, Peter continually and boldly claimed that he had never met Jesus. Jesus was being treated horribly by these people, and Peter turned away. Peter became afraid, and he acted as if he never knew Jesus. Take comfort that you have a Savior who understands. He understands because He has faced the same things you do, and He has overcome them all.

Prayer: Lord, give me the strength to be a good friend even if it costs me personally. Whenever someone forgets they know me, please help me to forgive them. Amen.

Journal: I'll Be Your Friend

When _____ turned on me, I felt _____
        (name)

_____

_____

_____

_____

_____

_____

When I am shunned by someone who is supposed to be my
friend, I react by _____

_____

_____

_____

_____

_____

_____

When I am let down by a friend, I will _____

_____

_____

_____

_____

_____

_____

_____

Encouragement: Your friend did what? (John 15:13)

That's Ridiculous | 48

Have you ever been laughed at for something you said or did? Maybe you told a story that was foolishness to those listening to you. Maybe you said something that embarrassed or made someone look bad, and the rest of the group laughed. Saying something awkward can be uncomfortable, but when you are serious about what you say, it can make you mad. Whatever the reason, being laughed at can make you feel ill or even mad. Luke 8:53: "And they began laughing at Him, knowing **they laughed at Him** that she had died." What this means is that Jesus understands what it is like to be laughed at. Jesus had arrived at the house where a little girl had died. Jesus told the crowd to stop crying for the girl. He said to them that the girl was not dead but asleep. The people thought this was absurd, so they laughed at Him. Take comfort that you have a Savior who understands. He understands because He has faced the same things you do, and He has overcome them all.

Prayer: Lord, sometimes I am taken the wrong way when I speak. Please help me to understand that people are not always going to agree with what I say. They may laugh at me, but You never will. Amen.

Journal: Keep Laughing

When _____ laughed at me for _____ ,

         (name)   (saying/doing what)

I felt _____

_____

_____

_____

_____

_____

When I am made fun of for what I say/do, I react by _____

_____

_____

_____

_____

_____

_____

When I am laughed at, I will _____

_____

_____

_____

_____

_____

_____

_____

Encouragement: Foolishness (1 Corinthians 1:25).

Gotta Work | 49

Do you have to work for a living? Maybe you are young and don't have to work yet, but some day, you will. Maybe you have worked to put yourself through school. If you have a family to support, you most likely have to work. Work is simply a part of life. Whatever the reason, work is a necessary requirement. Mark 6:3: "Is not this the carpenter, the son of Mary, and brother of James and Joses and Judas and Simon?" What this means is that Jesus understands what it is like to have a *built things* job. Yes, Jesus held a regular job. He started as *with His* an apprentice in His dad's carpentry shop, and *own hands* He became publicly known as a carpenter. Just like you, Jesus had a job title. Jesus, the carpenter, built things with His own hands. Take comfort that you have a Savior who understands. He understands because He has faced the same things you do, and He has overcome them all.

Prayer: Lord, sometimes work is difficult. Please help me to enjoy every aspect of my work and remember to be thankful. Amen.

Journal: Labor or Rest

When I work, I feel

_____

_____

_____

_____

_____

_____

When I go to work, I react by

_____

_____

_____

_____

_____

_____

As I continue to work, I will

_____

_____

_____

_____

_____

_____

_____

Encouragement: With all your heart (Colossians 3:23-24).

Don't Care | 50

Have you ever been accused of not caring? Maybe something happened to someone, and out of their trouble, they shouted at you, "You don't care about me." Maybe someone did not believe you were being empathetic to what they were going through, and you were charged with not being compassionate. You do care, but you are told you do not. Whatever the reason, being told that you do not care when you do can be frustrating. Mark 4:38: "Jesus Himself was in the stern, asleep on the cushion; and they woke Him and said to Him, 'Teacher, do You not care that we are perishing?'" What this means is that Jesus understands what it is like to be accused of not caring for His friends. Even though the others, on the boat, were worried, Jesus was not. Reading this in context, it is understandable that Jesus may have been exhausted from His work, and He was sleeping so deeply that He did not notice the storm. I find it interesting that Jesus was sailing with fishermen, but He was the one who was supposed to know what to do. They were annoyed by His demeanor, and they accused Him of not caring. Take comfort that you have a Savior who understands. He understands because He has faced the same things you do, and He has overcome them all.

Prayer: Lord, sometimes I am accused of not caring. Maybe sometimes they are right. Help me to be more caring, and help me to be understanding when I am accused of not caring. Amen.

Journal: I'm Concerned

When _____ accused me of not caring, I felt _____
      (name)

_____

_____

_____

_____

_____

_____

When someone says that I do not care, I react by _____

_____

_____

_____

_____

_____

_____

When I am charged with not caring, I will _____

_____

_____

_____

_____

_____

_____

_____

Encouragement: Silence every voice (Isaiah 54:17).

All Grown Up | 51

Were you ever a child? It is certain that no one is exempt from being a child before becoming an adult. Your childhood experiences, both good and bad, have shaped you into who you are now. We all must learn to advance in life. Ah, your very own bicycle; How awesome. Have you ever fallen and scraped your knee when you were learning to ride your bike? Remember those chores you had to do? Whatever the reason, childhood is filled with good and bad memories. Luke 2:40: "The Child (Jesus) continued to grow and become strong, increasing in wisdom; and the grace of God was upon Him." What this means is that Jesus understands what it is like to go through childhood. Jesus started life as a kid. Jesus had to grow up, just like you did. It is possible that He wanted to play just a little longer, but His mom interrupted Him by telling Him to come in and clean His room. He worked with His dad and learned to become a carpenter. Take comfort that you have a Savior who understands. He understands because He has faced the same things you do, and He has overcome them all.

Prayer: Lord, there are good things from my childhood, but there are others that I would rather forget. Please help me know Your truths of why these things happened. I am hopeful that good can come, even from the bad. Amen.

Journal: Keep On Growing

When _____ to me as a child, I felt _____

       (what happened)

_____

_____

_____

_____

_____

_____

When I think about _____ to me as a child, I

react by _____ (what happened)

_____

_____

_____

_____

_____

When I recall my childhood events, I will _____

_____

_____

_____

_____

_____

_____

_____

Encouragement: The plan works out (Romans 8:28).

Tolerance | 52

Have you ever had to tolerate stubbornness or ignorance? Maybe you had a child that continues to make the same mistakes no matter how many times you correct them. Maybe you commute to work, and your fellow commuters continue to cut you off. Maybe you work with people who are ignorant or lazy. Whatever the reason, having your tolerance pushed to its limits can wear out your patience. Luke 9:41: "And Jesus answered and said, 'You unbelieving and perverted generation, how long shall I be with you and put up with you?'" What this means is that Jesus understands what it is like to put up with people. Jesus asked how long will it take for them to see the light. Over and over, Jesus gave instruction and demonstrated what to do, but the people still gained no understanding. It must have felt like He was wasting His time. Take comfort that you have a Savior who understands. He understands because He has faced the same things you do, and He has overcome them all.

put up with people

Prayer: Lord, sometimes I run out of tolerance. Please give me Your wisdom and help me endure. Amen.

Journal: Take a Deep Breath

When I had to put up with _____, I felt _____

(name)

_____

_____

_____

_____

_____

_____

When I must tolerate someone's stubbornness or ignorance,
I react by _____

_____

_____

_____

_____

_____

_____

When I must tolerate someone, I will _____

_____

_____

_____

_____

_____

_____

_____

Encouragement: Patience, please (Romans 15:5 NLT).

Final Words

Jesus has always been God. Before, during, and after Jesus was on this earth, He was and is God. At the time when Jesus came, rather was sent into this world, He was the only Son of God. Those who have been born both of the flesh and of the spirit (born-again) are now also God's children by birth (John 1:12-13). All of this and much more made Jesus the Almighty God. He is all powerful, all-knowing, and eternal, with no beginning and no end. He is everything. However, one thing He was not until He was sent to this earth was a human. He came into this world as a baby. His body was formed by the Holy Spirit (Matthew 1:20), and He was born of a virgin (Matthew 1:18, Luke 1:27). Jesus was born as you were born. He cried when He was hungry. He was totally dependent on His parents to care for Him. Jesus did the things that you do. He ate, drank, slept, and faced many of the same challenges that you do. Jesus even died like you will one day. Once Jesus became a human, he began to understand what it was like to be human. Jesus walked the walk.

When Jesus was here on earth, He was all God as well as all man (Colossians 1:19). He experienced the things we do, but He did not completely understand (Mark 6:6) how you, as a sinner, relate to the world around you. At that time, it was impossible for Him to know life as you know life, even though He experienced many of the same things you do. Jesus was missing one thing that you have, and this single thing made Him different from you. Because of this one thing, Jesus could not fully relate to you, and He was bewildered about you because of it. Jesus lived His life on this earth, but He did not know what it was to have sin in His life (2 Corinthians 5:21). He did not have the nature of sin like you do. He knew no sin, and He could not sin because it was not in Him to do so. He did not know what it was to go against God's commands; therefore, He did not doubt God—not even once was He short of the mark. And then all of this changed. Jesus took all of your sin with Him to His death (1 Peter 2:24). He became sin, and He was the curse because of sin (Galatians 3:13). Jesus now understands what it is like to have sin in His life, and He understands what it is like to be abandoned by God because of the sin He carried. Yet through His resurrection, He overcame death, and He put sin away forever.

Now, Jesus understands everything. There is no stone left unturned. He understands you intimately and completely, yet His love for you has not changed; God's love never changes. His love has not changed, but the way in which He relates His love to you has. Jesus was always the Son of God, and He was the firstborn of God. As God, He is eternal, and as man, He was born, lived, and died. Jesus has always been and always will be God. Jesus is perfect as His Father is perfect. Jesus came to this world, and His coming to this world in no way made Him more or less God (Colossians 2:9).

Hebrews 2:17 says, "Therefore, He (Jesus) had to be made like His brethren in all things, so that He might become a merciful and faithful high priest in things pertaining to God, to make propitiation for the sins of the people." Jesus, the Almighty God, is the perfect High Priest who was able to give life and restore us to God the Father. Jesus did for us what we could not do for ourselves, but this was not enough. Jesus' coming to this world did something special. Before Jesus arrived here, the Lord was referred to as Shepherd. In Psalm 23, David says, "The Lord is my Shepherd." David spoke of a God who led him from afar. Jesus made shepherding personal (John 10:11, 14): "I am the good shepherd... " When Jesus came to know us in our humanity, He became a good shepherd who experienced our troubles. When Jesus took our sin on Himself at the Cross, His understanding of us became complete. He understands our life because He did it, and He understands our sin because He took it. Jesus is the GREAT Shepherd (Hebrews 13:20). Jesus understands you, and prepares you.

Let us pray. "Now may the God of peace, who through the blood of the eternal covenant brought back from the dead our Lord Jesus, that great Shepherd of the sheep, equip you with everything good for doing his will, and may he work in us what is pleasing to him, through Jesus Christ, to whom be glory forever and ever. Amen" (Hebrews 13:20-21).